Timothy Keller started Redeemer Presbyterian Church in New York City with his wife, Kathy, and their three sons. Redeemer grew to nearly 5,500 regular Sunday attendees and helped to start more than three hundred new churches around the world. In 2017 Keller moved from his role as senior minister at Redeemer to the staff of Redeemer City to City, an organization that helps national church leaders around the world reach and minister in global cities. He is the author of *The Prodigal Prophet*, *God's Wisdom for Navigating Life*, as well as *The Meaning of Marriage*, *The Prodigal God*, and *The Reason for God*, among others.

Kathy Keller received her MA in theological studies at Gordon-Conwell Theological Seminary. Kathy and Tim then moved to Virginia, where Tim started at his first church, West Hopewell Presbyterian Church. After nine years, Kathy and her family moved to New York City to start the Redeemer Presbyterian Church. Kathy cowrote *The Meaning of Marriage*, *The Songs of Jesus*, *God's Wisdom for Navigating Life*, and *The Meaning of Marriage: A Couple's Devotional* with Tim. *On Marriage* is their fifth collaboration.

On Marriage

TIMOTHY KELLER
and
KATHY KELLER

PENGUIN BOOKS

PENGUIN BOOKS
An imprint of Penguin Random House LLC
penguinrandomhouse.com

All Bible references are from the New International Version
(NIV), unless otherwise noted.

ISBN 9780143135364 (paperback)
ISBN 9780525507024 (ebook)

Printed in the United States of America
1   3   5   7   9   10   8   6   4   2

Set in Adobe Garamond · Designed by Sabrina Bowers

In memory of Dr. R. C. Sproul, who performed our wedding and got both our theology and our marriage going in the right direction

Contents

Introduction to the How to Find God Series

L ife is a journey, and finding and knowing God is fundamental to that journey. When a new child is born, when we approach marriage, and when we find ourselves facing death—either in old age or much earlier—it tends to concentrate the mind. We shake ourselves temporarily free from absorption in the whirl of daily life and ask the big questions of the ages:

Am I living for things that matter?

Will I have what it takes to face this new stage of life?

Do I have a real relationship with God?

The most fundamental transition any human being can make is what the Bible refers to as the new birth (John 3:1–8), or becoming a "new creation" (2 Corinthians 5:17). This can happen at any time in a life, of course, but often the circumstances that lead us to vital faith in Christ occur during these tectonic shifts in life stages. Over forty-five years of ministry, my wife, Kathy, and I have seen that people are particularly open to exploring a relationship with God at times of major life transition.

In this series of short books we want to help readers facing major life changes to think about what constitutes the truly changed life. Our purpose is to give readers the Christian foundations for life's most important and profound moments. We start with birth and baptism, move into marriage, and conclude with death. Our hope is that these slim books will provide guidance, comfort, wisdom, and, above all, will help point the way to finding and knowing God all throughout your life.

On Marriage

Beginning
a Marriage

Why bother to get married at all?

In the words of the traditional Christian wedding service, "God has established and sanctified marriage for the welfare and happiness of humankind."[1] While true, that cannot be the end of the discussion for modern people.

This is a more pressing question now than it has ever been in previous times. In the past it was a given that to become an adult member of society you married and had children, and the vast majority of people did so. But

younger adults in Western countries today post-
pone marriage at unprecedented rates. Nearly
a third of all millennials in the United States
may stay unmarried through age forty, and
25 percent may not marry at all, the highest
proportion of any generation in modern history.[2] Why? There are two reasons that so
many marriages never begin: economic stress
and the rise of individualism in culture.

Fears About Marriage

The economic factor is seen in the widespread
belief of single adults that they must be finan-
cially secure in a good career before they
marry and that, of course, their prospective
mate should be as well. The background assumption is that married life is a drain on

resources, especially with the arrival of children. Before marrying, it is therefore believed, you should have a guaranteed income stream, adequate savings, and perhaps even an investment portfolio.

However, this view flies in the face of both statistics and tradition. Traditionally, you got married not because you were economically secure and stable, but in order to become so. Marriage brings with it unique economic benefits. Studies show that married couples save significantly more than singles. Spouses can encourage one another to greater levels of self-discipline than can friends. Spouses also provide each other with more support through the trials of life, so that they experience greater physical and mental health than singles.

The other factor in the decline of marriage to which experts point is "expressive individualism."[3] This is a term popularized by sociologists to describe a growing cultural trend. In traditional cultures our personal identity was worked out in our relationships. "Who I am" was defined by my place in a family and community, and perhaps by my place in the universe with God. I became a person of worth as I fulfilled my responsibilities in these relationships. In modern times, however, we have turned inward. "Who I am" must not be determined by what anyone else says or thinks about me. I become a person of worth as I discover my own deepest desires and feelings and express them. Once I determine who I am, then I can enter into relationships, but only with those who accept me on my own terms.

This modern approach to identity is instilled in us by our culture in countless ways.

In the 2016 film *Moana*, the crown princess of a Polynesian island has been told by her father that she is the island's future leader and will have to submit to many traditional responsibilities. But instead, Moana has a desire to set out to sea to find adventure. Her grandmother sings her a song that tells her that her "true self" resides not in her duties and social responsibilities, but in the expression of her inmost desires. She tells Moana that if a "voice inside" her heart tells her to follow her desires, "that voice inside is *who you are*."[4]

We are assailed by this message at every turn—in television, movies, advertising, classrooms, books, social media, and casual conversation—until it is an unquestioned, virtually invisible assumption about how we become authentic persons.

The effect of this modern self on marriage has been considerable. It means that we do not want to even consider marriage if we have not established our own unique identity. We don't want anyone else to have any say in who we are until we have fully decided it for ourselves. Further, today we expect and even demand that all relationships be transactional, provisional as long as profitable, and never binding and permanent. If impermanence is the standard, then marriage and particularly parenting are deeply problematic since leaving a marriage is difficult and leaving a parenting relationship is essentially impossible. What if a relationship with a spouse or a child gets in the way of your expressing your "true self"?

Many modern people only marry if they believe they have found a spouse who won't try to change them and who will provide emotional and financial resources to help them toward their personal goals.

But it is an illusion to think that we find ourselves only by looking inside, rather than in relationships with those outside of us. In every heart there are deep, multiple, contradictory desires. Fear and anger exist alongside hope and aspiration. We try to sort these contradictory desires, determining which ones are "not really me." But what if they are *all* a part of me? How do we make decisions about which are "us" and which are not?

The answer is that we come to admire and respect some individuals or groups whose views we then deploy to sift and assess the impulses of our hearts. In other words, contrary to what we are told, we *do* develop an identity not merely by looking inside but through important relationships and narratives that profoundly shape how we see ourselves. We do *not* merely look within.

The traditional approach to marriage was wise, in that people knew intuitively that it would profoundly shape and reshape our identity. And that's good—because identity is always worked out in negotiation with significant others in your life. As psychologist Jennifer B. Rhodes put it, "In previous generations people were more willing to make that decision [to marry] and [then] figure it out."[5] What better way to discover who you are than to marry someone you love and respect, and then figure it out together?

So the contemporary decline in marriage is based on two mistaken beliefs about it, namely, that it is a drain economically and it is an im-

pediment to the full realization of our freedom and identity.

Marriage Was Made for Us

Social scientists have marshaled evidence against
these two mistaken views, showing how significantly marriage benefits us both economically and psychologically. In addition, they
have demonstrated how crucial the traditional family is to the welfare of the young,
that children do much better if raised in families of two married parents. But Christians
should not be at all surprised by these findings.[6] The book of Genesis tells us that God
established marriage even as he created the
human race. This should not be understood
to teach that every individual adult must be

married. Jesus himself was single, and since he stands as the great exemplar of what a human being should be, we cannot insist—as some cultures have—that you must be married to be a fully realized person. But neither can we see marriage, as our own culture does, as merely a development to guard property rights during the Neolithic Age that today can be altered or discarded as we please.

Wendell Berry famously addressed the modern idea that whether we have sex inside marriage or outside is "a completely private decision." He disagreed, saying, "Sex is not and cannot be any individual's 'own business,' nor is it merely the private concern of any couple. Sex, like any other necessary, precious, and volatile power that is commonly held, is everybody's business."[7] Sex outside of marriage creates babies outside of marriages, it often spreads disease, and it habituates us to treat others as pleasure objects rather than persons. All of these have a major impact on social conditions, conditions that affect everyone.

We know this line of thinking is deeply counterintuitive to modern people in the West, but it has been quite natural to most human beings in most places and times. Your choice regarding marriage is not ultimately a private decision. It affects everyone around you.

Marriage was made for us, and the human race was made for marriage.

Fear of Failure

There is another reason many people give to explain the modern reticence to marry. "I saw how difficult my own parents' marriage was, and I don't want that for myself." A fear of strife and marital failure keeps many people from seeking a spouse or, at least, makes them look for a prospective mate with virtually no flaws or personal weaknesses. Some people assume that if their parents divorced, their own future marriage is much more likely to end in divorce.

Joe Pinsker, in an article in *The Atlantic*, argues that not only does recent research show this is not true, but exposure to bad marriages can give you the resources to build a good one.[8] He gives the example of a man named Justin Lange. After his parents' divorce, Justin saw his mother remarry twice and his father three more times. He concluded that marriage was simply too hard and that he would never enter into it. But he met a woman, fell in love, and is now happily married after all. Why? "He attributes his present happiness . . . to going *against* the example his parents set."[9] He learned how to build a good marriage by *not* doing what they had done wrong.

Above all, he recognized his parents' biggest failure—to verbally make a lifetime commitment and then "not be willing to back it up." Divorce is sometimes necessary and the Bible allows for it. But longitudinal studies show that two-thirds of unhappy marriages, if they continue, become happy within five years.[10] Lange learned it was an illusion to believe that if he found the right partner they wouldn't fight like their parents did. He overcame the fear that marriage would be difficult. Of course it would be. He also overcame his fear that there would be fights. Of course there would be. But the secret is not to let these things weaken your commitment to love each other through it all. He said, "You may be upset about whatever mundane thing it is today, but is it going to matter later on? Just let it roll and focus on the important things."[11]

Misunderstanding Sex

There is another reason often given by both researchers as well as men themselves why males are less interested in marriage than in the past. Researchers point out that the ready availability of sex is one reason for the decline in marriage.[12] We have often heard men tell us the same thing directly: "It used to be that you pretty much had to get married to have a sexual relationship, but that's changed completely."

This attitude views sex as a commodity that used to be expensive. At one time you had to give up your independence through marriage in order to get sex. It was costly, but now it is available more cheaply, as it were. All such talk, however, conceives of sex as a physical and emotional experience that can be just as good if not better outside of marriage as it is inside.

From its very beginning, Christianity brought a revolutionary new understanding of sex into the world. It was seen as just one part—one uniquely joyful, powerful, and inseparable part—of mutual self-giving. To be loved and admired but not truly known is only mildly satisfying. To be known but rejected and not loved is our greatest nightmare. But to become vulnerable and so fully known and yet accepted and fully loved by someone we admire—that is the greatest possible satisfaction. In marriage, spouses lose their independence and so become vulnerable and interdependent. They do not hold themselves back so that they only relate temporarily, provisionally, and transactionally. They give their entire selves to each other—emotionally, physically, legally, economically.

The startling sex ethic of the early Christians was that sex is both a sign and a means for that total self-giving, and that it must not be used for any other purpose. To engage in sex for any other reason was to misunderstand it. Granting access to our physical bodies must be accompanied by the opening of our whole lives to each other through a life-long marriage covenant. Only in that situation, the early Christians taught, does sex become the unitive and fulfilling act it was meant to be.

This new sexual code of "no sex outside of marriage" startled the Roman world because it seemed highly restrictive.[13] But it actually elevated sex from a mere commodity of pleasure into a way to create the deepest possible bond and community between two human beings, as well as a way to honor and resemble the One who gave himself wholly for us so we could be liberated to give ourselves exclusively to him.

> Flee from sexual immorality . . . Do
> you not know that your bodies are

temples of the Holy Spirit, who is in you, whom you have received from God? You are not your own; you were bought at a price. Therefore honor God with your bodies. (1 Corinthians 6:18–20)

Like the citizens of ancient Rome, modern people see the biblical sex ethic as restrictive and unattractive. And yet there are signs and evidences that the supposed outdated Christian view still resonates with our deeper intuitions about sex.

Superconsensual Sex

A woman writing in *The New York Times* described a sexual encounter with a man she had met on Tinder. She was nearly thirty and he was twenty-four, an age difference that did not seem significant until he began "asking for my consent about nearly everything."[14] He asked if he could take her sweater off and after she said yes he also asked if he could take off her tank top, then her bra. She snorted that he didn't have to ask permission for every little thing. "A dramatic shift" had taken place in the "sexual training" of younger men, leading them to repeatedly ask for verbal consent. After it was all over, she said, "In fact I had liked it as a form of care-taking. I just wasn't used to being taken care of in that way."[15] It had felt very intimate.

Later, however, when she texted him, he did not answer; he simply "ghosted" her. When she told her roommates how hurt she was, they couldn't understand. "Because he

asked for my consent, over and over," she explained, "sex felt like a sacred act, and then he
disappeared." They didn't understand why she
was so hurt but,

> . . . in the days and weeks after, I was
> left thinking that our culture's current
> approach to consent is too narrow . . .
> Consent doesn't work if we relegate it
> exclusively to the sexual realm. Our
> bodies are only one part of the com-
> plex constellation of who we are. To
> base our culture of consent on the
> body alone is to expect that caretak-
> ing involves only the physical. I wish
> we could view consent as something
> that's . . . more about care for the
> other person, the entire person . . .

Because I don't think many of us would say yes to the question "Is it O.K. if I act like I care about you and then disappear?"[16]

If what the Bible says about God's design for marriage and sexuality is true, then this woman's experience is not surprising. Giving our bodies to each other without giving our whole lives fails to recognize the integrated nature of the self. The body can't be separated from the whole. Sex should indeed be a reciprocal offering of each other's lives, and to give your body to someone who feels free to leave afterward and not care for you is dehumanizing.

Christians have the deepest and broadest understanding of consent possible. When

Christians say that sex is for marriage only, they mean sex must be superconsensual.

Seeking Marriage Well

So how do you begin a marriage? Most readers would answer: by seeking and finding someone to marry, obviously. But that answer is a modern one. In past times spouses were provided to you by families. Even a hundred years ago, although you made your own choices, your options were limited. Most people lived in smaller communities. You had to select a spouse from a fairly small pool of people, and virtually all of them could be evaluated over years, through face-to-face interaction.

All that has changed. Now if you go on dating apps such as OkCupid, you join 30 million other users. The number of potential partners is dizzying and the challenge of choosing among them can be paralyzing. Even if you get over your fear, however, the very mode of evaluating thousands of people not by face-to-face experience but online can reshape marriage seeking into a shopping experience. Persons are reduced to consumer products as you compare their height, weight, looks, and so on.

The problem is that even without social media we were always too prone to operating in this way. It is instinctive for a single person to walk into a room of other singles and to implicitly eliminate as prospective partners anyone who does not make the cut on the basis of physical and financial factors. Once we have eliminated them, we take a second look at those left in our pool and evaluate for things like character and a feeling of "connection" or affinity. The problem is that you have already ruled out people who may have the character and affinity you seek.

Social media and dating apps only accentuate this self-defeating strategy many times over. One major problem is that the people you are looking at online are providing you a highly filtered representation. You are looking for character and connection, but as one researcher points out: "There is no evidence that you can assess that online." Instead, says Eli Finkel of Northwestern University, online misconceptions are rampant. "You think you know what you want but what you really need is to sit across from each other and get a beer."[17]

Does this mean you should not try to meet

people online? Not necessarily, but the only way to proceed is to, first, resist the "shopping experience" approach to marriage seeking that eliminates people based purely on the physical and financial and, second, find ways to "sit across from each other" and get to know them.

Once we find ways to sit across from someone, what are we looking for?

1. *Look for another believer, if you are a Christian.*

At first glance this seems like a statement of prejudice, but if someone does not share your Christian faith that means that he or she does not understand it. And, if your faith is at all important to how you think and live, it means they don't understand you either. Surely the essence of a good marriage is someone who "gets" you, but if someone doesn't share your faith, they can't. The only way to let such a relationship grow in intimacy is if you make Jesus more peripheral in your daily thinking and feeling.

2 Corinthians 6:14 urges Christians not to be "unequally yoked" in our closest relationships with people who don't share our deepest beliefs. The image is of a farmer trying to yoke together two different animals—say an ox and a donkey—who were of different heights, weights, and gaits. The heavy wooden yoke, instead of harnessing the power of the team to do the task, would rub and chafe *both* animals. So a marriage between someone who is a practicing, believing Christian and someone who is not can be unfair and painful to both partners.

2. *Look for someone who will still attract you when they lose their youthful looks.*

While physical attraction must grow between married partners, it should be based on a deeper sort of attraction. In the Bible book Song of Solomon, the lover says, "You have stolen my heart with one glance of your eyes" (Song of Solomon 4:9). As much as this book of the Bible rejoices in sexual love, the part of the body that gets the most attention from the lovers is the other person's eyes. And this is not so much a focus on the loveliness of their physical shape; the "glance" of the eyes reveals the character and personality of the lover. Indeed, when bodies are aging and losing their loveliness, the glance of the eyes can be even more thoughtful and wise, more joyful and loving. To be captivated by someone's eyes is a way of saying you are attracted to the person's heart.

Romantic attraction should not ignore physical looks, but it must not be the most important part, because no one keeps their looks over the long haul. Paul tells us in 2 Corinthians 4:16 that even as their bodies become weaker and older, believers can be growing stronger and more beautiful internally. The more we fix our gaze on the loveliness of our partner's inward being, the more our physical attraction will grow even as our physical attractiveness lessens over the years.

3. *Finally, get advice from others about your relationship before you proceed to marriage.*

In the past it was unlikely that you would enter into a romance with someone your family and friends didn't know. Feedback about your partner came naturally from many people who knew you as well as him or her. Today we are mobile people living on our mobile phones. We move from place to place. Many who actually see us in person every day are people who don't know us well. Meanwhile many of the people who have known us the longest are distant and can only "see" us through filtered representations online. Many of our most longtime associates are in the dark about how we are really doing.

The result is that we make more decisions in a vacuum, including decisions about romance and marriage. But marriage is too important a choice to be made without counsel, and there are married couples with the accumulated wisdom and experience from whom you need to hear. Take advantage of this wisdom and seek advice from the married couples in your life.

Starting Marriage Well

Once you marry, how do you begin to lay the foundation for a long, rich marriage?

In advance of our marriage Kathy was told numerous times that her wedding day would be "the happiest day of her life." We sincerely hoped not! Every day following the wedding has been a day in which we moved forward in understanding each other and in adjusting to and serving each other. Every day has been one more day to learn and enjoy better the fruits of repentance and forgiveness.

Our attitude might have had something to do with an offhand comment by R. C.

Sproul, the minister who performed our marriage service. He said, "Vesta and I have been married for fifteen years now, and we think we're just about getting the hang of it." At first glance that might seem like an intimidating statement—fifteen years of marriage and they were *still* just getting the hang of it? But now, from the vantage point of our forty-five years of marriage, we are inclined to think he underestimated how long it takes to learn each other's heart and life rhythms, to practice self-denial in the service of the health of the relationship, and to grow in the knowledge of alien (someone else's) love languages. But whether the learning curve is long or short, any marriage must begin well in order to be built better. We have considered a few (not the only) important foundational habits, practices, behaviors, and attitudes that should be established at the outset.[18]

1. ***Never go to bed angry.*** It's become a cliché, but there is a strong biblical reason behind it. This follows Saint Paul's direction to "not let the sun go down on your anger" in Ephesians 4:26. That means that rather than repress and hide your unhappiness, you and your spouse must become adept at a new skill set. Those skills include: First, you must express what is bothering you in a way that is truthful but not an attack. Second, you must learn to sincerely repent for how you've hurt your spouse but do so by neither excusing yourself nor engaging in so much self-shaming that your spouse just says, "Forget I brought it up." Third, you must learn how to give and to receive forgiveness.

In medical circles it is widely believed that

sleep is the time when what is learned and ex-
perienced during the day becomes organized
into memories and habits. If you go to bed
angry at your spouse, you will nourish an attitude of resentment. If you do it enough
times, it will grow into a deeply felt anger,
even hatred. How does one avoid going to
bed angry? See number 2.

2. *Pray together as your last words of the
   day.* One can hardly pray in anger (not
   very easily, anyway), and even if all you do
   is spend five minutes petitioning God for
   his blessing on your family and your lives,
   you will have to relinquish your anger in
   order to enter God's presence.

3. *Give each other sex often.* This would seem
   like a no-brainer to newlyweds! However,

sexual energy is like all other energy, and when you are tired it is easy to forget or put off sex for "a better time." Lack of intimate touching can lead to distance between spouses. We use the word "give" intentionally. All of us have fallen into the myth that wild flights of passion possess each partner simultaneously, when the truth is that usually one person is more interested in sex than the other. On those occasions, the less-interested spouse can *give* sex as a gift. Saint Paul, himself a bachelor, makes this into a culture-challenging biblical command:

> The husband should fulfill his marital
> duty to his wife, and likewise the wife
> to her husband. The wife does not

have authority over her own body but yields it to her husband. In the same way, the husband does not have authority over his own body but yields it to his wife. Do not deprive each other except perhaps by mutual consent and for a time, so that you may devote yourselves to prayer. Then come together again so that Satan will not tempt you because of your lack of self-control. (1 Corinthians 7:3–5)

In a world where men had all the sexual privileges, Paul insists that husbands and wives have equal rights over each other's bodies, and that it is not a good thing to "deprive" each other unless it is by mutual consent, and then for only a short period.

4. ***Make deliberate decisions about your family life and traditions.*** You will have grown up observing your parents or other adults in their roles as men and women, husband and wife, parents, grandparents, and so on. You will have no choice but to unconsciously carry those prototypes with you into your own marriage. *That* is how a husband treats his wife. *This* is the way we celebrate holidays. Vacations *always* mean going to the beach. These assumptions will affect your life together in the big things and in the small, so it is best to make them conscious, examine them, and decide as a couple how your new family unit will do things.

When we got married, Kathy brought with her the image of a father who cooked

Saturday breakfast so his wife could sleep in, and who could change a diaper with the best of them. (With five children he had gotten plenty of practice!) Tim, on the other hand, had lived in a family where his father had to be at work at 5:00 A.M., returning exhausted in the evening. Beyond providing for his family, he was not asked to contribute in any way. Shortly after our first son was born, Tim's parents took him aside, worried that he was being "henpecked" because Kathy had asked him to change a diaper. He firmly said, "Mom and Dad, thanks for your concern, but in our family we do things differently than you did." Opening gifts on Christmas Eve or Christmas morning? You decide together. Music or TV turned on first thing in the morning, or not? (Kathy let out a screech when Tim turned on the radio the first

morning we awoke in our apartment together! Should have discussed that one!)

We are not discussing the odious practice
of negotiating every chore and keeping score
to see who fulfills their bargain. We have
talked about male and female roles in marriage at length elsewhere. We're talking about
creating new traditions that fit your new family, rather than making assumptions about
how things are done based on your family of
origin.

5. Finally, *learn each other's "love languages."* One of the most important
   books we ever read was Judson Swihart's
   How Do You Say "I Love You"?[19] Early in
   the book he gives an illustration of a
   German-speaking man saying *"Ich liebe*

dich" to a girl who speaks only French. He is loving her but she doesn't feel the love because he is literally not conveying it in a language she can understand. That's natural, he writes, because "most people only speak those languages they themselves understand."[20]

He goes on to argue—quite rightly, in our experience—that each of us has certain ways we want love expressed to us. In our pre-marital counseling, R. C. told this story from his own marriage as an illustration. For his birthday he was hoping for a new set of golf clubs, something he would not have bought for himself. However, his practical wife, Vesta, got him six new white shirts. When her birthday came around he surprised her with a fancy new coat, sure she would be delighted, but what she really wanted was a new washing machine. They had missed each other's love language, speaking only their own.

For us, when Tim proactively helps Kathy with her domestic duties around the house, that is much more emotionally valuable to her than when he verbally says how much he loves her, or even when he buys her a gift. In other words, when he "says" he loves her in that way she feels much more loved than if he expresses it some other way. He's speaking her language. Swihart and others give you a whole list of "love languages": spending time together, meeting emotional needs, saying it with words, saying it with touch, being on the same side, bringing out the best in each other, and others. It is crucial to discover your spouse's most valued languages and become fluent in them even if they are not similarly important to you.

Discuss, agree, and begin to do these five things, and your marriage is off and running!

Sustaining a Marriage

The Bible begins with a marriage in Genesis and ends with a marriage at the wedding supper of the Lamb in Revelation. The Christian understanding is that marriage points us to God and the gospel—but at the same time it is the gospel that gives us the greatest possible resources for marriage. Here's the first marriage depicted for us in Genesis, chapter 2.

> The LORD God said, "It is not good for the man to be alone. I will make a

helper suitable for him." Now the LORD God had formed out of the ground all the beasts of the field and all the birds of the air. He brought them to the man to see what he would name them; and whatever the man called each living creature, that was its name. So the man gave names to all the livestock, the birds of the air and all the beasts of the field. But for Adam no suitable helper was found. So the LORD God caused the man to fall into a deep sleep; and while he was sleeping, he took one of the man's ribs and closed up the place with flesh. Then the LORD God made a woman from the rib he had taken out of the man, and he brought her to the man. The man said, "This is now bone of my bones and flesh of my flesh; she shall be called 'woman,' for she was taken out of man." For this reason a man will leave his father and mother and is united to his wife, and they will become one flesh. The man and his wife were both naked, and they felt no shame. (Genesis 2:18–25)

Let's look at this passage to learn what we need for a good marriage over the long run, over decades. It speaks to us of three things we have to have.

Avoidance of Idolatry

It is customary in weddings for the bride to walk to the groom, often accompanied by her

father or both parents or someone else. Genesis 2 shows us that the tradition stretches
back to the garden of Eden. In this case it is
God who is doing the honors, drawing the
wife to the husband.

And when Adam sees Eve, he speaks po-
etry, the first recorded in the Bible. In most
Bibles it is printed on the page indented and
in verse form. The man explodes into song at
the sight of his wife.

His first Hebrew word means "At last." It
can also be translated "Finally!" He is saying,
"This is what I've been looking for. This is what
has been missing." But what is it? He says that
she is "bone of my bones and flesh of my
flesh." It's a way of saying "I have found myself
in you. At last, by knowing you I can know
myself." Remember that Adam is speaking
from paradise, where he has a perfect relation-

ship with God. Yet finding a spouse and partner speaks to something so profound in us that
Adam erupts in adoration through artistic expression. This points to an important fact that
we must understand if we are going to have a
successful marriage over the long term.

John Newton, who is best known as the
writer of the hymn "Amazing Grace," was
also a wise pastor in eighteenth-century Brit-
ain. He wrote a series of letters to a young
couple just starting out in marriage. He often
counseled newlyweds, saying that you may
think that having a bad marriage is the biggest problem you may face. However, a good
marriage can be every bit as big a spiritual
danger. He writes:

> With such an amiable partner, your
> chief danger perhaps will lie in being

too happy. Alas! the deceitfulness of our hearts, in a time of prosperity, exposes us to the greatest of evils, to wander from the fountain of living waters, and to sit down by broken cisterns. Permit me to hint to you, yea, to both of you: Beware of idolatry. I have smarted for it; it has distressed me with many imaginary fears, and cut me out much cause of real humiliation and grief. . . . The old leaven,— a tendency to the covenant of works, still cleaves to me.[1]

What is he talking about? He is using biblical imagery. Cisterns were open tanks made of stone or lime plaster that were used in ancient times to collect rainwater for use by people in their homes. But if the cistern was cracked, the water leaked out, leaving no remedy for thirst. "Broken cisterns" (Jeremiah 2:13) was a metaphor that the prophets used to describe how we look for our deepest satisfaction and security not in God, but in things of this world. Jesus told the woman in Samaria that the only source of final satisfaction was not in romance and marriage but in him (John 4:14), the source of "living water."

Newton is saying that good marriages run the great risk of turning your heart from God to your spouse as a greater source of love, safety, and joy. Not only that, Newton speaks of a good marriage as the cause of backsliding into a "covenant of works." What does that mean?

A "covenant of works" is an old theological term for a system in which you earn your salvation through your performance. You say to yourself, "The reason God will bless me and take me to heaven is that I'm living a good life and I deserve it." The Christian gospel is completely opposed to this mind-set. We are told, "For it is by grace you have been saved, through faith—and this is not from yourselves, it is the gift of God—not by [our good] works, so that no one can boast" (Ephesians 2:8–9).

John Newton as an Anglican minister knew this through and through, at least in his head. But, practically speaking, the idolization of his wife and marriage led him to slip back into a covenant of works. And that can happen to us. You will look to your spouse to give you the things only God can really give you. You can look to your spouse's love, your spouse's respect, your spouse's affirmation to give you a sense of your own value and worth. In other words, you will be looking to your spouse to save you. You are, in a sense, slipping back into the covenant of works.

This is easy to do because marriage is such a great thing. And it is easy to turn a great thing into the ultimate thing in your life.

As Newton says, it has led to many fears, humiliation, and grief. How? You put intolerable pressure on your spouse to always be healthy, happy, happy with you, and affirming. Yet nobody can bear the weight of that level of expectation. Criticism from your spouse can crush you. Problems with your spouse can devastate you, too. If anything at all goes wrong with your partner, your life may begin to collapse. And if your spouse dies, how can your "god" comfort you with love when he or she is in the coffin?

So what can we do? You must not try to lessen your love for your spouse or the person you think you're going to marry. Rather, you have to increase your love for God. C. S. Lewis says it is probably impossible to love any human being too much. You may love him too much in comparison to your love for God, but it is the smallness of your love for God, not the greatness of your love for the person, that constitutes the inordinacy. Marriage will ruin us unless we have a true and existential love relationship with God.[2]

Traditional societies believe you're nobody unless you're somebody's spouse, but the Christian faith was started by a single man. Saint Paul, in 2 Corinthians, says essentially, "You want to be married? Great. You're not married? Great." Paul means the relationship every single Christian has with God through Christ is so intimate and the relationship Christian brothers and sisters have inside the family of God can be so close, that no one who is single should be seen as having a life without family connections or as missing out on the greatest love of all.

So the first thing we need for a *great* marriage, paradoxically, is to see its penultimacy. But that's only the first thing we need.

Patience for the Long Journey

In Genesis 2:18 we read: "The LORD God said, 'It is not good for the man to be alone. I will make a helper suitable for him.'" The Hebrew word *"ezer,"* translated as "helper," is regularly used in the Bible to refer to military reinforcements. Imagine you are a small troop overwhelmed by far greater enemy forces. Suddenly you see reinforcements rushing in to strengthen you in the battle. Think of your relief and joy! Without them you would have been defeated. That's the sense of the word here, and it is often used of God at places in the Bible. "Helper," then, does not mean "assistant," but rather someone who has a supplementary strength that you don't have. That is the word used for the woman, the wife in the first marriage relationship.

But there's another word—"suitable." Some have rendered this verse "I will make a helper *fit* for him." The King James translation famously has God saying, "I will make him an help *meet* for him." That's why "helpmeet" was a traditional (but now largely opaque) term for a wife.

Yet we should dig deeper for the full meaning of the original verse in Hebrew. Where the verse is translated as "I will make a helper suitable for him," there are actually two Hebrew words in the sentence that are translated by "suitable." The Hebrew literally says, "I will make a helper *like opposite* him." Our first impression is that this is a contradiction—is it "like" or is it "opposite"? But it clarifies things to think of two pieces of a puzzle. Two pieces of a puzzle fit together not if they are identical and not if they are randomly different. They only fit perfectly and form a whole if they are *rightly* different, different in a way that both corresponds yet complements.

God is sending into Adam's life (and therefore, God is also sending into Eve's life) someone with enormous power, but with a power
that is different. "Like opposite," whatever else
it means, means noninterchangeable. Each
gender has excellencies and glories, perspec-
tives and powers, that the other does not have.
In marriage, a person of a different gender
comes into your life—a person who is profoundly, mysteriously different.

Many people have tried to define masculinity and femininity with a list of specific char-
acteristics. But as soon as you try to list them,
you will find that they do not fit people in all
cultures, nor even of all temperaments. Most
important, the Bible does not give us a list of
male and female traits. Yet gender differences
are assumed in the Scripture, not least here in

Genesis 1 and 2. The message of the text is that only together, armed with the whole array of masculinity and femininity, are you going to be able to handle life as a married couple. The military background of the word "help" hints at this. Only together do you have what it takes not to be defeated.

We—Tim and Kathy—do not fit the gender stereotypes. We think it's fair to say that by traditional standards Tim is not very masculine and Kathy is not extremely feminine. Yet we had not been married long before we began to realize that we often saw the world very differently, and those differences couldn't all be chalked up to temperament or family or class or ethnicity. For example, Kathy was startled by Tim's ability to put his feelings and fears to one side in order to focus on the task at hand. While as a woman she of course was also more than capable of single-mindedness, Tim went about it in a very different way. Kathy saw things in Tim he would never have seen; she sees them because she's a different gender yet is close enough to notice.

As the years have gone by, we can see more ways that our marriage has made us like the two puzzle parts interlocked and forming a bigger whole. Now when things happen to Tim and he has a split second to react, he is conscious of what Kathy would think, say, or do in this situation. Tim has tangled with his wife so often that her perspective has been instilled in him. That means his repertoire of possible responses no longer includes only his own, but hers as well. In that split second he can think, *I know what Kathy would do, and is that a more wise and appropriate action than my habitual way?* And often now he does things the Kathy way.

You see, his wisdom portfolio has been permanently diversified. He's a different person, and yet he's still himself. He hasn't become more feminine. In fact, probably in many ways he's become more masculine as time has gone on. What's going on? Kathy came into Tim's life, and now he not only understands who he is better through her eyes, but he's grown. He's become who he is supposed to be only through the daily interactions, often painful, with a person who's like him, not him, opposite to him, in close.

Perhaps it does not need to be said—but we should say it anyway—that the husband is also to be a help to his wife. It's not just Eve who's brought into Adam's life with her gender resources to help him be who he's supposed to be. In Ephesians 5:25–27 it says that husbands should love their wives sacrificially as Christ loved us, and for the same purpose, to help our wives become radiant and beautiful, overcoming their faults and flaws. In a sense that's Genesis 2 in reverse. Husbands are to use their gender-differentiated resources to help their wives become who God made them to be, just as wives are to help their husbands.

But this all assumes a long journey, a drawn-out process. People do not change and become who they are meant to be overnight. We are to use our different gifts and to love each other sacrificially to help each other grow and thrive all through our lives.

It is fair to say that this is not the view of marriage that is on the rise in our culture.

Today we are consumers. Consumers are always instinctively doing cost-benefit analysis. The logic of the market, of investing and buying and selling for profit, has invaded every area of our lives, including marriage. So we look for a spouse who meets our needs, who is not high-maintenance, who won't try to change us, and who is compatible in every way. If we get into marriage with someone "like opposite" to us, who begins telling us things about ourselves we don't want to hear, we say, "This isn't right. This is supposed to be blissful. Why are we always having these confrontations?" The answer is—because you are getting *help*. And only on the far side of this discomfort will you find the person God wants you to be.

Now these first two things we need—the avoidance of idolatry, and patience for a long, sometimes difficult journey—could be seen as opposite problems. On the one hand, you have to avoid a romantic naïveté that puts your spouse on a pedestal. On the other hand, you have to avoid the anger you feel at how much work it is to love someone so different, who tells you things you don't want to hear. In Greek mythology Ulysses had to navigate his boat between the opposite sea monsters Scylla and Charybdis. If you got too close to one monster, the great danger was that you would overcorrect your course and steer into the reach and power of the other. Certainly many people have abandoned marriage idolatry only to land in the arms of deep disillusionment.

What does it take to avoid both "monsters"? How are we going to avoid expecting too much or too little from marriage?

The Joyful Humility
Only the Gospel Can Give

Genesis 2:18 says, "The LORD God said, 'It is not good for the man to be alone.'" That is a surprising statement. Why would Adam be lonely and unhappy in paradise, before there was any sin in the world? He had a perfect relationship with God; how could he be lonely? There's only one possible answer, really. God deliberately made it so that Adam would need someone besides God. That doesn't mean, of course, that our heart's *supreme* need for love isn't God. It is. What it does mean is that God designed us so that we also needed human love.

Consider what a humble, unself-centered act this is on God's part. God made human beings to need not just him, but other relationships, other selves, other hearts. The belief that God made people so he wouldn't be lonely, or so that he'd have someone to love (like having a child), or because he needed worshippers, is patently false. Yet it is nothing compared to the humility and sacrificial love God shows us later in the Bible when he says repeatedly through prophets such as Isaiah, Jeremiah, and Hosea, "I am the bridegroom, and you, my people, are the bride."

The "bridegroom" language means that solely in God do you have the lover and spouse that will satisfy you supremely. He's the ultimate "helpmeet." Martin Luther wrote about this when he said:

> A mighty fortress is our God, a bulwark never
> failing;
> Our helper He, amidst the flood of mortal ills
> prevailing

He is our help in the midst of all "mortal ills" because he is like-opposite you. He's like you because you're created in his image—you're personal and relational, as he is. But he's not like you because he's perfectly holy. You'll never become the person you're supposed to be unless he comes into your life. And to call him our "bridegroom" means he cannot be merely some entity you believe in abstractly, or even just a deity whose rules you obey. There must be intimacy in your relationship. There must be interaction. He must speak to you through his Word and you must pour out your soul to him in prayer and worship. His spousal love must be shed in your heart through the Holy Spirit (Romans 5:5). The only way you will ever avoid making an idol and savior out of your human spouse is if God is in your life as your bridegroom.

The imagery of "bridegroom" also means that in God you have the most patient and long-suffering spouse who ever existed.

The theme of God as the bridegroom of his people runs all through the Bible. In the Old Testament, of course, God calls himself the husband of Israel. But Israel constantly turned to worship other gods and in so doing she is spoken of as being guilty of spiritual adultery. Jeremiah 2–3 and Ezekiel 16 are vivid depictions of this "bad marriage," but the most famous exposition of this theme is in the book of Hosea. There God tells his prophet to marry Gomer, a woman who will be unfaithful to Hosea, "for like an adulterous wife this land [Israel] is guilty of unfaithfulness to the LORD" (Hosea 1:2).[3] And this is what happens. She goes after other lovers.

The most famous and poignant part of the story comes in the third chapter. Gomer has not only been unfaithful, she seems to have fallen into prostitution, because the only way Hosea can get her back was to purchase her from a man who owned her. God tells Hosea to do just that. Hosea writes:

> The LORD said to me, "Go, show your love to your wife again, though she is loved by another man and is an adulteress. Love her as the LORD loves the Israelites, though they turn to other gods and love the sacred raisin cakes." So I bought her for fifteen shekels of silver and about a homer and a lethek of barley. Then I told her, "You are to live with me many days; you must

> not be a prostitute or be intimate
> with any man, and I will behave the
> same way toward you." (Hosea 3:1–3)

This is more than just a moving story of indefatigable love. God is hinting that, just as it requires costly self-sacrifice to love a wayward spouse, so his love for us, if it is going to be maintained, will entail cost and sacrifice on his part as well. And in Jesus's life and death we see that taken to its logical conclusion.

When the religious leaders in Matthew 9 asked Jesus, "How is it that . . . your disciples do not fast?" he replied, "How can the friends of the bridegroom mourn while he is with them?" Fasting was a religious rite that was accompanied by repentance and prayer. Jesus answered with an illustration that relied on the obvious fact that when you go to a wedding party you don't fast. (You may even go on a vacation from any diets.) But when Jesus called himself *the bridegroom* the listeners must have gasped. Everybody knew that the bridegroom of Israel was the Lord God himself—and that was who Jesus was claiming to be. Then Jesus added: "The time will come when the bridegroom will be taken from them; then they will fast" (Matthew 9:15). So he was saying two things about himself—first, that he is our divine bridegroom, and second, that he has come to die for us, to be taken away.

What the book of Hosea was hinting at we see writ large in the New Testament. God is the lover and spouse of his people. But we have given him the marriage from hell. God is in the longest-lived, worst marriage in the history of the world. We have turned to idols in our hearts, we have turned away from him, we have been absolutely terrible spouses. But God did not abandon us.

In Jesus Christ, God entered the world and paid the price to buy us away from our sin and enslavements by dying on the Cross. In essence, God says to us in the Bible: "In Jesus Christ I laid down my life for you. I did cosmically and visibly the thing that you have to do every time you try to love somebody who is flawed and imperfect. It was a substitutionary sacrifice. Your sin, your evil, your problems came onto me so that my righteousness could be put on you. Do you understand that? Now you understand how much I love you. Now you understand my delight in you." That message is the most life-changing, potent power in the world.

See how, if we rest in this reality, it gives us the greatest possible encouragement for the long journey of marriage? Remember that Jesus came to "his own" but his own received him not (John 1:11). We didn't just spurn him; we nailed him to the Cross. Some of you may be in bad marriages and may think, "Oh, my spouse is crucifying me," but in God's case it really happened. Yet Jesus loved us not because we were good, but in order to make us good. He loves us for *our* sakes, not for his sake, and so he stayed and loved us. Whenever you are ready to give up on a difficult spouse, remember Jesus's patience with you. In order to really stick with a marriage you need over and over and over again to look at your spouse and say, "You wronged me, but I wronged my great spouse, Jesus

Christ, and he kept covering me and forgiving me, so I'm loved enough by him that I can offer the same thing to you." That's the only way you'll have patience for the journey.

And, circling back, the knowledge of Christ's spousal love is also the key to the avoidance of idolatry. In Martin Luther's classic essay "On the Freedom of a Christian," he writes:

> The third incomparable grace of faith is this, that it unites the soul to Christ as the wife to a husband . . . [T]hen it follows that all they have becomes theirs in common, as well good things as evil things, so that whatsoever Christ possesses, that the believing soul may take to itself and boast of as its own, and whatever belongs to the soul, that Christ claims as his . . . Let

faith step in, and then sin, death, and hell belong to Christ, and grace, life, and salvation come to the soul. For if he is a husband, he must needs take to himself that which is his wife's, and, at the same time, impart to his wife that which is his . . . [Therefore] by the wedding ring of faith . . . the believing soul . . . becomes free from all sin, fearless of death, safe from hell, and endowed with the eternal righteousness, life, and salvation of our husband Jesus Christ.

Who can value highly enough these royal nuptials? Who can comprehend the riches of the glory of his grace? . . . From all this you will again understand why so much importance is attributed to faith, so that it alone can fulfill the law and justify without works.[4]

Luther is right that no one can "value highly enough these royal nuptials," and yet we must try. We must daily think about, savor, relish, and rejoice in Christ's spousal love to the point of growing delight. That will free us from idolizing the human love we need from our spouse; it will also give us "grace, life, and salvation" that only can be found in Jesus himself. This spouse, Jesus Christ, is the only spouse who's really going to save you. He's the only one who can really fulfill you.

Your marriage to him is the surest possible foundation for your marriage to anyone else.

The Destiny
of Marriage

Then I heard what sounded like a great multitude, like the roar of rushing waters and like loud peals of thunder, shouting:

> *"Hallelujah!*
> *For our Lord God Almighty reigns.*
> *Let us rejoice and be glad*
> *and give him glory!*
> *For the wedding of the Lamb has come,*
> *and his bride has made herself ready.*
> *Fine linen, bright and clean,*
> *was given her to wear."*

—REVELATION 19:6–8

Then I saw "a new heaven and a new earth," for the first heaven and the first earth had passed away, and there was no longer any sea. I saw the

Holy City, the new Jerusalem, coming down out of heaven from God, prepared as a bride beautifully dressed for her husband.

—REVELATION 21:1-2

M arriage is a journey that traditionally has been said to have an ending— "till death do us part." In one sense death certainly does end a marriage. The surviving spouse is free to marry again, for example. Yet the Christian understanding is that marriage prepares us for an eternal union of which our earthly marriage was only a foretaste. And even the relationship two Christians have in marriage here in this world need not be seen as something that is ended or even diminished by death.

To understand the true destiny of marriage, we need to look at sex, at the goal of history, and at the resurrection itself.

The Signpost of Sex

Many people have pointed out that the Bible is not a prudish book. It is often celebratory about the beauty and pleasures of sexual love, as seen in the verses in Proverbs 5:18–20 that tell a husband to be ravished with his wife's breasts, or the entire book of the Song of Solomon. But the Bible goes beyond frankness, and even fun, when it talks about sex. It goes to glory.

In Romans 7 the apostle Paul likens Christians to a woman who has been married "to the law." That is, we have been trying to save ourselves by our performance—whether that means religious observance of God's moral law or the pursuit of wealth, career, or some cause. But when we believe in Christ we become married "to him who was raised from

the dead, that we might bear fruit to God"
(Romans 7:4). This is a daring image. As a
wife puts herself into the arms of her husband, and children are born into the world
through her body, so we put ourselves in the
arms of Jesus and then we also bear fruit—of
our own changed lives (Galatians 5:22–23) or
of good works that change the lives of others
(Colossians 1:6, 10).[1]

Some commentators have struggled with
Paul's imagery here, calling it "undignified,"
and indeed it is somewhat breathtaking.[2] But
the metaphor seems clear enough. In some
sense married sexuality, which can create new
life, points to the ultimate love relationship
with Jesus Christ. Union with him by faith
gives us the supreme experience of love, which
can in turn bear transformative, life-generating

fruit. That relationship, as Paul says, begins now, and so can the fruit bearing. But the Bible tells us elsewhere that the communion with Christ and his love that we have now is only a very dim hint of what it will be like to see him face-to-face (1 Corinthians 13:12).

The Bible tells us that we currently know our Spouse only by faith, not by sight (2 Corinthians 5:7). The love we experience here can only ever be partial. But when we actually see him face-to-face, the transformation of his love and the fulfillment of our being will be complete (1 John 3:2–3).

What do all these passages about Jesus being our husband and bridegroom mean? It means at least this—that sex in marriage is both a pointer to and a foretaste of the joy of that perfect future world of love. In heaven when we know him directly, we enter into a union of love with him and all other people who love him. On that great day there's going to be deep delight, towering joy, and deep security of which the most rapturous sex between a man and a woman is just an echo.

As we saw before, 1 Corinthians 6 tells us that sex outside of marriage is wrong. But in this text Saint Paul does not merely give a bare prohibition—he explains *why* it is wrong for a Christian.

> Whoever is united with the Lord is one with him in spirit. Flee from sexual immorality . . . Whoever sins sexually sins against their own body. Do you not know that your bodies are temples of the Holy Spirit, who is in you, whom you have received from

God? You are not your own. (1 Corinthians 6:17–19)

Paul reminds us (as in Romans 7:4) that we are married to Christ, and so the Holy Spirit comes to dwell in us. Therefore, he reasons, we must not do anything sexually with our bodies that does not reflect and mirror that relationship to him. When we unite with Christ we give ourselves wholly and exclusively and permanently to him, as he sacrificed himself for us. In the same way we must never have sex apart from giving our whole lives, exclusively and permanently, to a spouse. Any other use of sex fails to let it be what God made it to be: a signpost of our union with him, present and future.

That's what the Bible teaches about sex, and that goes far beyond just "sex positivity."

Many people today were raised being told that "sex is dangerous and kind of dirty." Then people started to overcorrect for that by saying, "Sex is a good thing that brings pleasure and fulfillment, and you can use it anyway you want as long as it's consensual."

The Bible's vision for sex is infinitely higher than either of these views, and it is not anything in the middle. Sex is not dirty—it was made by God and he pronounced it "good" (Genesis 1:26–31). But sex is far more than just an appetite such as eating.

The glory of God in the face of Jesus is the beauty and love we have been looking for all our lives. "In your face is fullness of joy; in your right hand are pleasures forevermore" (Psalm 16:13). We will finally know the fulfillment of our natures, the infinite satisfaction of his presence (Psalm 17:15).

Will that day be pleasurable? Of course. And that's why sex, its earthly analogy, is fun and pleasurable. But sex can be far more than a momentary thrill if we align it in time and space with what it points to in the future. We must use it as a way to say to someone else: "I belong completely, exclusively, and permanently to you." When we do that, it becomes not a way to get pleasure from someone, but a deeply unitive act, a way to cement two human lives into a single entity and community, and a way to shape your heart so as to love sacrificially as Jesus loved us. Only in the context of marriage does sex reach its complete potential to delight and fulfill.

So sex, like marriage itself, points to something beyond itself. If we don't see that and set our hearts on that future, sex and marriage will always bitterly disappoint us.

The End of History

As Luther says, in keeping with Saint Paul's views, we are in one sense already married to Christ. But there is another sense in which we are not yet married—we are more like engaged to him. Revelation tells us "the marriage supper of the lamb" is a future day in which we will be married to Jesus (Revelation 19:7). The great wedding day in which we fall into his arms is the only wedding day that will really make everything right in our lives.

It is significant that the Bible begins in Genesis with a wedding, and that wedding's original purpose was to fill the world with children of God. But Adam and Eve turned from God and the first wedding failed to fulfill its purpose.

When we come to the end of the Bible we

see the church "coming down out of heaven from God, prepared as a bride beautifully dressed for her husband." The echoes of Genesis 2 are unmistakable. Again we see God bringing a bride to her husband, only this time the husband is Jesus and we are the bride. In that first marriage Adam failed to step in and help his wife when she needed him. But at the end of time there will be another wedding, the marriage supper of the Lamb, and *its* purpose is also to fill the world with children of God. *It* will succeed where the first marriage failed because, while the first husband in history failed, the Second Husband does not. The true Adam, Jesus Christ, will never fail his spouse, the Second Eve, his church.

Let's also notice something new that was not mentioned in Genesis. It says that we, his people, will be dressed beautifully for our husband. Of course the primary reason there is no mention of a wedding dress in the Garden of Eden is that Adam and Eve were "naked and unashamed." That was, however, before the coming of sin. The Bible often talks metaphorically about our need to have our sin covered by clean or beautiful garments (Psalm 32; Ezekiel 16; Zechariah 3). If we are to be beautiful to our husband, we will have to have our sins covered by his grace and righteousness (Philippians 3:9). And the image of the wedding dress conveys this in a wonderful way.

Wedding garments are designed to make us feel beautiful—like our best possible selves. These clothes are a great metaphor for how Jesus covers our sins and clothes us in his righteousness, at infinite cost to himself. The gospel is that Christ lived the beautiful and good life that we should live but have not. But now, by faith, his beauty rests upon us. When we believe, we get his righteousness, as Martin Luther explained. Revelation tells us that we, in a sense, will come down the aisle to Jesus and we will look beautiful to him. Can you grasp how astonishing that is?

As a minister I have had the privilege of standing beside the groom in hundreds of weddings. My wife and I always watch the groom in the moment before the arrival of the bride. You can tell *exactly* when he catches sight of her as she comes through a doorway or turns a corner and suddenly—there she is. The groom catches his breath and his heart leaps when he sees her looking so radiant. The radiance on his face echoes hers as they gaze on each other.

Is the Bible really saying that Jesus finds us beautiful like that? That we will have that kind of love from the Lord of the universe? Yes. This is what it means to be "in Christ," what it means to belong to him. Of course we can only partially comprehend this intellectually and experientially. 1 John 3:2 says: "Dear friends . . . what we will be has not yet been made known. But we know that when Christ appears we shall be like him, for we shall see him as he is." The first sight of his beauty and glory, and the first direct experience of his love, will immediately transform us into spotless persons of "freedom and glory" (Romans 8:21). That's in the future, of course, but then John adds: "All who have this hope in him purify themselves just as he is pure" (3:3). This future beatific vision and wedding supper will be so powerful, John says, that to even hope for it—to get the barest foretaste of it and to rest in our assurance of it—begins to transform us now.

As we rejoice in the spousal love of Jesus we will be changed. Fears, jealousies, resentments, boredom, disillusionments, loneliness— all the things that darken our lives—will diminish. And only if you look beyond the end of your earthly marriage to your union with Christ will you love your husband or wife well.

You must shed the illusion of thinking, "If I can just find *the one* and get married, then my life will be OK." No. There is only one "the One," and he awaits you at the end of time, at the feast. When you see his glory it will make up for a million terrible lifetimes.

And the beauty he will put on you that day will outshine the best wedding dress you've ever seen.

The End of Marriage?

In Matthew 22 we read of the Sadducees, a party of leaders in ancient Israel who did not believe in a future resurrection of the dead. They knew Jesus believed and taught it and so they tried to trap him. They presented a hypothetical case. There were seven brothers and the first one married a wife. He died, however, and she married the second brother. Then he died, and she married the next brother. On this went until she had married all seven men and they all died. "Now then," they concluded, "at the resurrection, whose wife will she be of the seven, since all of them were married to her?"

Jesus began his answer by saying, "You are in error because you do not know the Scriptures or the power of God" (Matthew 22:29). Not only did they not know the Bible, but their God was too small. They had no true sense of his infinite wisdom, glory, and love. They couldn't really imagine him creating much of a different world than the one we have now.

As for the teaching of the Bible, Jesus says:

> "Have you not read what God said to you, 'I am the God of Abraham, the God of Isaac, and the God of Jacob'? He is not the God of the dead but of the living." (Matthew 22:31–32)

God never says, "I *was* the God of Abraham, Isaac, and Jacob." Though it was centuries after their deaths when he spoke these words to Moses (Exodus 3:6), God never speaks about them as if his relationship with them was in the past tense. "I *am* their God," the Lord says, and Jesus adds, "God is not the God of the dead but of the living." In other words, no one who has the true God as their God is ever really dead. One biblical scholar explained Jesus's saying this way: "Those with whom the living God identifies himself cannot be truly dead, and therefore they must be alive with him after their earthly life is finished."[3] In this Jesus establishes the general principle that to unite with God through faith is to be destined for a greater life beyond the end of this one.

Then Jesus says, speaking directly to the

Sadducees' hypothetical case: "At the resurrection people will neither marry nor be given in marriage; they will be like the angels in heaven" (Matthew 22:30).

At first, this seems to mean that death is, indeed, the end of our marriages. Certainly, in the resurrection we will be "like the angels" in that there will be no need for procreation in order to replenish the population. There will be no death, and so we can imagine why an institution that was largely dedicated to the birth and nurture of new life would not be necessary.

But R. T. France, in his commentary on Matthew, poses a question that hangs in the air as we hear Jesus's words. He writes: "Those who have found some of the deepest joys of earthly life in the special bond of a married relationship may be dismayed to hear that

that must be left behind." However, France notices that Jesus's terms "marry" and "giving in marriage" are two verbs that refer to the custom of the bride's father giving a bride away and to the act of the bridegroom in receiving her. In other words, Jesus is saying that the active pairing off into marriage will not continue. Then France adds:

> But note that what Jesus declares to be inappropriate in heaven is marriage, not love. [Why couldn't it be that] heavenly relationships are not something *less* than marriage, but something *more*[?] He does not say that the love between those who have been married on earth will vanish, but rather implies that it will be broadened so that no one is excluded."[4]

C. S. Lewis in *The Four Loves* speaks of a close trio of friends—Jack (C. S. Lewis), Ronald (J. R. R. Tolkien), and Charles (Charles Williams). When Charles died, Lewis noticed that he did not as a consequence get "more" of Ronald. The things in Ronald that only Charles could draw out were now lost to Jack. In other words, the more he shared Ronald's friendship with others, the more of it he had himself. Lewis concluded that this was a faint image of the perfect love relationships we will have in heaven, when jealousy and selfishness will be gone.[5]

So in the question posed by the Sadducees, which of the brothers will the woman be married to in the resurrection? The answer is— she will be wife to all of them and then some. (This is a good answer to hear if you have had a spouse die and have subsequently had another good marriage.) The answer is everyone will be in the closest possible love relationship with everyone else, because Christ's perfect love will be flowing in and out of us like a fountain, like a river.

Will we still be with our earthly spouse in heaven, in the resurrection? Certainly. Look at Jesus, the first born from the dead. When he encountered people he knew, as on the road to Emmaus in Luke 24, he had been changed enough that they did not know him at first, and yet then they recognized him. He was still himself, though now with a perfect, resurrected body. His friends were still his friends.

And who better than your spouse of many years will be able to rejoice in your new resurrected self? When all your sins and flaws are removed from your soul and body your spouse will be able to say with infinite joy, "I always knew you could be like this. I saw it in you. But now look at you!"

In the letter by John Newton to newly-weds cited earlier, he writes about the relationship we will have with each other beyond death:

> So sure as you are joined you must part, and such separations are hard to flesh and blood; but it will only be a separation for a little time. You will walk together as fellow-heirs of eternal life, helpmeets and partakers of each other's spiritual joys, and at length you shall meet before the throne of glory, and be for ever with the Lord. May you live under the influence of these views, and find every sweet made still

sweeter by the shining of the Sun of Righteousness upon your souls; and every cross sanctified to lead you to a nearer, more immediate, and more absolute dependence on himself.[6]

The end of your earthly marriage will be nothing less than an entrance into an endless feast, where you will be joined to your earthly partner in ways you could never realize in this world, as well as with all others and with Jesus, "Lover of your soul."

Acknowledgments

For this book and the series of which it is a part, we owe even more thanks than usual to our editor at Viking, Brian Tart. It was Brian who saw the short meditation on death that Tim preached at the funeral of Terry Hall, Kathy's sister. He proposed that we turn it not only into one but three short books on birth, marriage, and death. We also thank our many friends in South Carolina who made it possible to write this and the companion books while at Folly Beach last summer.

Notes

Beginning a Marriage

1. From "The Order for the Solemnization of Marriage" in the Presbyterian *Book of Common Worship* (Philadelphia: Presbyterian Board of Publication, 1906), and Genesis 2:22–24.

2. Belinda Luscombe, "Why 25% of Millennials Will Never Get Married," *Time*, September 24, 2014, time.com/3422624 /report-millennials-marriage/.

3. See Robert Bellah et al., *Habits of the Heart: Individualism and Commitment in American Life* (Berkeley and Los Angeles, CA: University of California Press, 2007).

4. "Where You Are," lyrics by Mark Mancina and Lin-Manuel Miranda, from *Moana* (2016). This is ironically a very Western, individualistic approach to identity being awkwardly superimposed on a (fictional) girl in a non-Western culture. That is

certainly within the scope of artistic license, but it's fair to point out that it is an example of how contemporary Western secular people think of their worldview as a universal truth that can improve the cultures of the rest of the world.

5. Jennifer B. Rhodes, cited in Marissa Hermanson, "How Millennials Are Redefining Marriage," Gottman Institute, *Gottman Relationship Blog*, July 3, 2018, www.gottman.com/blog/millennials-redefining-marriage/.

6. Just one sample of many studies: W. Bradford Wilcox, "The New Progressive Argument: For Kids, Marriage Per Se Doesn't Matter," Institute for Family Studies, September 15, 2014, ifstudies.org/blog/for-kids-marriage-per-se-doesnt-matter-right/.

7. Wendell Berry, "Sex, Economy, Freedom, and Community," *Sex, Economy, Freedom, and Community* (New York: Pantheon, 1993), 119.

8. Joe Pinsker, "How Successful Are the Marriages of People with Divorced Parents?" *Atlantic*, May 30, 2019.

9. Pinsker, "How Successful Are the Marriages of People with Divorced Parents?" I added the italics in the quotation.

10. Linda J. Waite et al., "Does Divorce Make People Happy? Findings from a Study of Unhappy Marriages," Institute for American Values, 2002, http://www.americanvalues .org/search/item.php?id=13.

11. Pinsker, "How Successful Are the Marriages of People with Divorced Parents?"

12. Paula England, "Is the Retreat from Marriage Due to Cheap Sex, Men's Waning Job Prospects, or Both?" Institute for Family Studies, November 1, 2017, ifstudies.org/blog/is-the -retreat-from-marriage-due-to-cheap-sex -mens-waning-job-prospects-or-both.

13. Kyle Harper, *From Shame to Sin: The Christian Transformation of Sexual Morality in Late Antiquity* (Cambridge, MA: Harvard University Press, 2016), 86. Also see all of Harper's chapter 2, "The Will and the World in Early Christian Sexuality," 80–133.

14. Courtney Sender, "He Asked Permission to Touch, but Not to Ghost," *New York Times*, September 7, 2018.

15. Sender, "He Asked Permission to Touch, but Not to Ghost."

16. Sender, "He Asked Permission to Touch, but Not to Ghost."

17. Quoted in Carolyn Kaufman, "Why Finding a Life Partner Isn't That Simple," *Psychology Today*, April 20, 2013.

18. Caveat: If you have been living together before marriage (and I hope you have not, as that is not a good preparation for marriage), these suggestions still apply to you. See Timothy and Kathy Keller, *The Meaning of Marriage* (New York: Penguin, 2011) Introduction. Living together is very different from actually being married. The knowledge that "the back door is always unlocked" and can be used if anything goes really sour means that you don't have to stick around for the hard work of relationship building, problem solving, and family nurturing.

19. Judson Swihart, *How Do You Say "I Love You"?* (Downers Grove, IL: InterVarsity Press, 1977). A much more well-known and recent popular book on this subject is Gary Chapman's *The 5 Love Languages: The Secret to Love That Lasts* (Chicago: Northfield Publishing, 2010).

20. Swihart, *How Do You Say "I Love You"?*, 15.

Sustaining a Marriage

1. John Newton and Richard Cecil, *The Works of John Newton*, vol. 6 (London: Hamilton, Adams & Co., 1824), 132–33.
2. C. S. Lewis, *The Four Loves* (New York: HarperCollins, 2017), 157.
3. For a major study of the theme of "God as our spouse," see Raymond C. Ortlund Jr., *God's Unfaithful Wife: A Biblical Theology of Spiritual Adultery* (Downers Grove, IL: IVP Academic, 2003).
4. Text from *First Principles of the Reformation*, ed. by Henry Wace and C. A. Buchheim (London: John Murray, 1883), can be found at https://sourcebooks.fordham.edu/mod/luther-freedomchristian.asp.

The Destiny of Marriage

1. "The Fruitful Bride" in Francis Schaeffer, *True Spirituality* (Wheaton, IL: Tyndale House, 2001), 72–81.
2. See the discussion by John Murray, *The*

Epistle to the Romans, single-volume edition (Grand Rapids, MI: William B. Eerdmans, 1971), 244, and especially n7.

3. R. T. France, *The Gospel of Matthew*, The New International Commentary on the New Testament (Grand Rapids, MI: William B. Eerdmans, 2007), 840–41.

4. France, *The Gospel of Matthew*, 839.

5. C. S. Lewis, *The Four Loves* (New York: HarperCollins, 2017), 78–79.

6. John Newton and Richard Cecil, *The Works of John Newton*, vol. 6 (London: Hamilton, Adams & Co., 1824), 132–33.

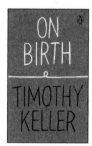

ON BIRTH

If life is a journey, there are few events as significant as birth, marriage, and death. In *On Birth*, bestselling author Timothy Keller explains the deeper Christian understanding of birth and baptism.

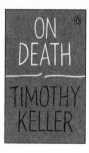

ON DEATH

In a culture that largely avoids thinking about the inevitability of death, Timothy Keller celebrates the Christian resources of hope in the face of death. Slim and compelling, *On Death* gives us the tools to understand God's triumph over death through the work of Jesus.

PENGUIN BOOKS